COULD I...
SHOULD I...
WOULD I..
HOW DO I..

FORGIVE...

by: Pamela Cotton

Would I...

Should I...

Could I...

How Do I...

Forgive?

Pamela Cotton

Top Shelf Publications
Milwaukee, Wisconsin USA

Top Shelf Publications

Would I...Should I...Could I...How Do I...Forgive?

Copyright © 2008 by Pamela Cotton

Edited: Sonja Williams

For all who heed the call to accept a wonderful, astounding, marvelous change in your life while positioning yourself to experience genuine, indisputable, real peace and authentic, true liberty…This book
Is for
You.

Contents

Part 4
How Do I...

Part 5
Forgiving

Preface

Between gunshots, blood shed ongoing feuds (vendettas), we most times say, "My, this world is in a terrible condition."

To prepare for the evening news, requires a box of Kleenex tissues and a pill to calm your nerves. Sometimes it becomes so devastating until you must simply flip quickly to another channel or just hit the off button and opts for a piece of chocolate.

Most negative interpretation of what we see, hear, taste, and feel is a direct residual of "_unforgiveness_." I have a dispute against him or I have an ought against her, how about, they caused me strife! They hurt me, and now they are going to pay!

Nevertheless, look we cannot reward evil for good! We can no longer side – step, and skirt around the edges of what the truth of our down – fall. Some are searching to know the truth. However, far too many are evasive.

Most feel a lack of empowerment. You would think that we have had our fill of destructive situations, living on the edge in wait in order to take revenge. Listen to your heart, child. Come out from among your own self-disillusions. You are not an island. All of us are just wonderful little pieces mud!

This book, *Would I...Should I...Could I...How Do I...Forgive?*, is a guide that gives you real life experiences that will take you step by step to another level in your life. After you read this book honestly *apply* the basic principles to your life, you will feel lighter on you feet, you will be inspired to run and tell others who... *Would I...Should I...Could I...How Do I...Forgive?*

Gerthene Jasper-Thompson

Forward

When I first realized that God had a plan of salvation that offered humanity the forgiveness of sin, I was elated! I thought His forgiveness was the ultimate gift and it was. To think that the God of the Universe has made provisions to unconditionally forgive our every sin was mind blowing to say the least.

I have since realized that the God-given ability to forgive others is extremely advantageous and has proven to be a great gift as well; a gift that we have somehow overlooked. I find that many people forget or just refuse to practice the fine art of forgiveness. To our own dismay, we treat the command to forgive others as an option, and we suffer greatly as a result.

After reading *Would I…Should I…Could I…How Do I…Forgive?* I realized how important and essential it is to practice forgiveness daily. It should be the 11th commandment! What joy, what peace, what happiness, what healing we often forfeit when we refuse to set aside our pride and forgive any and all offences that come our way? Sounds difficult? It Is! Nevertheless, you have to ask yourself the real question "is the choice to forgive worth the trouble? The answer, "You bet it is!

After reading this book I give credence to, you will be inspired to walk in forgiveness and watch God's power transform your life and the lives of those that surround you. There is POWER in FORGIVENESS! Enjoy.

Marilyn Morrow – Cotton

Acknowledgements

Thank you Father God, in the name of Jesus for inspiration and an irreplaceable support system. I want to give special thanks to my Mommy, (LeDora Cotton) My wonderful son Allen LaShun Cotton, Sheryl, Carl, Gladys, Marilyn, Elder Minnie Bellemy, Girt, Dr. Johnson, Marsha, Dad (Jefferson D. Goudy), Bonita, Cheray, Mother Annie Love, and Sister Debora, for insight beyond compare. I love y'all so much and I know I have told you many times, because I really mean it from my heart and soul. Thank you, Sonja and Laron Williams. You're so easy to love, thank you. May God continue to cover, protect, prosper, crown your head with His wisdom (applied) and bless you all.

Introduction

Life is full of uncertainties – the ups and downs, the "good ", the" bad" and yes the "unknown". From the moment we are old enough to discern the difference between having our own personal, physical and emotional needs met or un-met, we run the risk of falling into the trap of un – forgiveness, of judging someone for not behaving in the manner we desire – thus setting ourselves up in a state of mind that may control our destiny in more ways that can be imagined.

This topic focusing on forgiveness or Un – forgiveness forever profoundly important in the lives of everyone – young and old, male or female, gay or straight – it simply does not matter who we are, we face this question and oftcn find it difficult to make the choice. The author,

Pamela Cotton has chosen to title her book (Would I...Should I...Could I... How do I...Forgive?) Her title was no doubt, based on sigifiant heart – wrenching chapters in her life in which "forgiveness" or "un - forgiveness" was a question to be pondered and wrestled with before making a full decision on how to proceed one way or the other

The terms, "forgiveness" and "un – forgiveness are discussed in many discourses. In fact they are frequently discussed throughout out biblical scriptures as well as secular literature, particularly in literature dealing with "personal development" concerns (Johnson, 1990). When reviewing biblical text, the term, "forgive" as it relates to our selves and others is cited a number of times in both Old and New Testament (Holy Bible – New International Version (NIV Matthew). For example, "The Lord's Prayer" as found in the book of

Matthew speaks directly to "forgiveness" for ourselves and for others as well, "forgive us our debts as we forgive o our debtors…"Many people across this country and around the world, pray this prayer daily. However whether or not they actually forgive others is indeed questionable.

Despite the magnitude of scriptures supporting the need to forgive others, author Cotton raises the issue: "Would I...Should I…Could I… How do I, forgive?" The discussion of a series of explicit circumstances not only Cotton's pass but others allows us to understand the need to ponder over the question at hand. In many instansnces our ability and willingness to forgive depends somewhat on our level of trust in people and society in general. Most of us human beings need to believe that life will be "fair" to us at least somewhat "fair". We need to believe others will not completely invade our space, our humanity, our sense of physical and emotion safety. Author Cotton, discusses instances in which all of these basic privileges and protections were invaded and some literally destroyed.

From the eyes and mind of a young girl, Cotton brings the reader to tears when she describes family situations both physical and emotional abuse, and pain inflicted upon herself and others. She discusses not only" general abuse" (if there is such a thing), but family issues in detail. These life – altering circumstances cross cut those incidents inflicted by individual will as well as those that fall under the auspices of political, economic, historical, social and racially charged agendas. Certainly, most of us already know the close relationship between abuse through individual will and the residuals of the later.

The author has not only provided cases of her own situons and struggles with forgiveness, she also gives the reader cases in which others she knew struggled with issues that placed "Forgiveness" in question. For example, she describes the life of a strong Christian woman her "God-Mother" who although relied on God for most things, was placed in a position in which she was forced; threw in her pride and for a time and prayed hard in order to release him.

Un – forgiveness for some one who had wronged her. Cotton should be commended for her willingness to be so transparent and candidly describe these painful events. With helping others to unravel and come to grips with their own painful situations and circumstances, she has helped so more of us learn the healing power of "forgiveness" and ultimately freedom.

As you read Pamela's book you will be enticed to think of a time or times when you have been faced with situations in which you wonder if you could forgive someone; or if you should even consider forgiveness. Maybe the pain was too deep that you feel to forgive is out of the question. Maybe you have escaped this issue altogether and have never been hurt to the point in which" not to forgive." was a question for you.

Author Cotton not only talks about forgiveness, but also gives clear directions and instructions on how to overcome and implement ("FORGIVENESS")

Florence L. Johnson, Ph.

How to approach this book:

"How Do I Forgive"

You *can* forgive people who don't care; you can forgive *yourself*, people who hurt you, and others. Forgiveness *is* possible.

As a man thinketh ...so is he. You can be entertained or informed, but the real goal here is to move you to higher level in your consciousness and ultimately in your life. This book speaks to thousands, millions, actually all men, or shall I say all human species.

The truth is where you will find answers that will benefit you and cause you to grow in life. As you consume this book with active enjoyment keep in mind, growth is possible, self - improvement is posible, forgiveness is possible. Ask question, affirm, visualize and verbalize as you take this journey.

If you think you can, you can! My friend often says, "You have what you say!" I found that to be factual. If at first you don't succeed, learn from it and try again...proceed! Refuse to have your life punctuated with short-comings. To fail at anything gives us a unique opportunity to re–think our life's plan...then, proceed. Forgiveness, true forgiveness is a process. Forgiveness is possible.

Pamela Cotton

Do You Hear What I Hear?

I talked to my sister, Sheryl
Phillips Goldsberry Cotton, and my
sister–n–law Marilyn Morrow-Cotton,
about this work …this forgiveness
"thang" and they shared some things with
me about their experiences. I am sure if
you are breathing; you too have had some
experiences that have called you to

consider whether to forgive or not to forgive. Anyway, I asked them to give me some excerpts from their experiences concerning this very fine "*life-metamorphosizing*" topic. Ok…life-changing experience! There! (Smile) After they agreed, I got all excited inside because I knew them personally and I knew they would have the substantial prudence to constrain your attention.

Also, I have interviewed many people on my quest to offer you, the reader, some contrasting points of view, and some real assistance, help, or information in making a positive change in your life. And if you are challenged to any degree to implement forgiveness, this book will point you in the right direction for sure! Then you can get on with living a life that is unfettered and totally free.

I was fervent to do this work because of many of my friends and relatives along with yours truly (ha – ha) have experienced a real problem with this issue of forgiveness. Many times we say we have, and have not. We say, we do, and do not. We pray that we learn to walk in forgiveness, yet we pick up the offence again like a bad habit and act like we have never even tried to exercise forgiveness.

Sometimes we just don't know how to forgive. And so I would like to encourage some and admonish others who are at the crossroads of the healing adventure of: dat – da –da dah… "Forgiveness"!

___

"Forgiveness is an absolute necessity for continued human existence"
! Archbishop Desmond Tutu

___

Everybody has a story. Everybody has some problematic issue or situation that plagues their existence. How big is your problem, really? Is it only all about you…Your house, your neighborhood, your city, your state, your country, your continent, your world, your universe!?"

In reality our problems are very minuscule in comparison to the situations the world is facing. Talk about thinking inside the box! Will you allow that thing that happened to you stop your progress? If forgiveness is the key to a fulfilled, joyful and peaceful existence, will you forgive? (Pc)

Note: Often times we already know the answers too many of life's challenges and our personal problems.

We really do know how to be healthy, but we still eat the wrong things, smoke, and drink excessively and do not exercise. Now here is the difference between successful people and unsuccessful people. Successful people do! Unsuccessful people only think about doing!

Successful people get up early and yes; they do get out of their beds and *do*! They put things in action! However the unsuccessful person just lay there with good intentions! Do you know somebody who watches exercise programs on TV, but never actually get involved and do the exercise?

We become reckless because there are no immediate results! We become reckless with our bodies, minds, health, marriages and financial concerns. (Selah) Likewise, we don't forgive because there are no immediate results.

Truth is, forgiveness can rescue a crumbling marriage, family aggravation, and it can also start a physical healing process. Who wouldn't want to be healed and made whole?

This reminds me of a man who sat impaired at the side of the healing pool for 38 long years. For 38 years when the angel stirred the pool, he sat there and for some reason refused to enter in. For 38 years he remained an invalid. So close to his miracle but yet so far. And he complained, "I had no one to put me in the pool."   He said that every time, and someone always got in before him. He was full of excuses.

Then I heard a modern commentator say, "I would have scooted, crawled, or just simply rolled over an inch at a time just to fall into that healing pool!"   Ha, ha – ha! Hindsight is always 20/20 but the idea here is to *do* something to improve your quality of life. Sitting on excuses won't solve any problems. You must take action to improve your quality of life. Lead or follow…but do something!

Now let's *Do This*! It is possible!

I was inspired to do this work after observing many people who would tell of a time in their life when they had to forgive someone. I talked with one lady and while she began telling her story she started sweating and deep breathing and began trembling. When she finished I ask her when did this happen? She replied, "25 years ago"! But I recall she told it as if it happened yesterday. I asked her if she forgave. She said she had forgiven that person. I thought, 'I can't tell'.

I have a known a young man for over 40 years. He was very smart and very talented. I watched him grow up and become happily married and they had three beautiful children.

He began to cheat on his wife and bring home sexually transmitted diseases. They argued, fussed and fought. Most of the time financial challenges induced these bouts of tension. His wife stayed with him and endured many things. Most would not have lasted one year, not to mention seven years or more.

He began to use drugs and his life took a spiral downhill. Soon his wife divorced him and all of his sons found themselves in the penal system. The last time I saw him, he told me that he could never forgive himself for destroying his family.

Talent wasted, he travels from pillar to post, still looking for peace and contentment. His sons have many years ahead of them in prison. His wife has moved on but there is still pain and resentment. I can't help but wonder what could have happened had he just managed to forgive, himself! Forgiveness is powerful.

Part 1:

Would I...

Chapter 1

Never Again

The night sky was full of twinkling stars and the wind ushered in a chill of 20 degrees below zero. The wind was furiously blowing and whistling. The wind chimes on the porch made melody that demanded one's attention. The neighborhood was quiet and you could smell the fragrance of smoke that poured from the many surrounding chimneys. It was normal night at our home.

The children were in their room listening to music and playing video games, and every so often I would glance at the TV in the living room while doing dishes in the kitchen. All of a sudden, the lights went out and a loud noise was heard throughout the house. Louder than the blazing sound of the TV in the living room, louder than the music that blasted from the kid's room. Then there was silence as two men appeared.

They demanded that we all come into the children's room and lay on the floor. As they bound my hands with duct tape, I was overcome with intense fear and my main concern was for my kids. I screamed, "Please don't hurt my children"! A deep voice came from behind the mask, "Shut up! Then came the duct tape over my mouth as they began to tie up my children.

Soon the men were not in sight. Everything got foggy and I thought they left. I then heard them talking in another room but I couldn't make out what they were saying. They ram-shacked the house looking for things of value. I couldn't help but give due consideration to the possibility of their murderous intentions. I pondered what I could do. I managed to reach in my pocket and retrieve my cell phone. I had forgotten to put it on charge, but thank God I was able to use my chin to push the speed call to my husband's cell phone. Then it dawned on me as I heard his phone ringing in the other room. His phone was here at the house. I then called 911 on my speed dial, but I couldn't talk. At that time one of the men, moving swiftly entered the room, put his foot on my head and took my phone away.

All of a sudden there was a knock at the door. It was my neighbor, Mary. She just started calling my name. She called me with every fiber in her being. I'm telling you, she was very persistent. I have never before or since heard her call me like that. When the intruders heard her voice, they ran out of the back door. Thank God for nosey neighbors. She said something sounded funny at our house and she sensed something was wrong. Her loud annoying voice saved our lives!

The police were called and they did an extensive investigation. What we discovered changed my life forever. They detected the only things missing were jewelry and my coin collection, which had a total value of about $1500.00.

The sorrowful but revealing truth is that the investigators discovered my husband's involvement. They determined *he* was one of the men that perpetrated this horrifying invasion against me and my family. As it was revealed, he had a hidden drug problem for quite some time. He put our lives in danger to secure drug money!

I often ask myself why didn't I see this, where were the signs? Did I disregard the signs?! Could I ever forgive him for this? I hated him, I just hated him! Whenever I thought about him my blood boiled, I would become tense and furious all over again.

"It hurts! I'll never trust anybody to that degree again! NEVER!" This is what I uttered in the silence of my bedroom. No one was there; my husband that I made a vow to love, cherish and obey was gone. Tears streamed down my face pouring across the bridge of my nose. Holding my head in the palm of my hands I felt as if it were going to burst open.

I developed a deep depression and entertained thoughts of suicide. Feeling hopeless and full of despair, I knew my life would never be the same. "It's nothing" I said audibly, "I've been through more drama than this and I survived." But inwardly I was devastated. I had no one. My mother never really cared about me, my father ran off years ago and the only one that did love me unconditionally was grandma, and she was dead. I hated this man because I felt as though he played me and put my life and the life of my children in danger. Forgiveness was not an option.

This young lady would not let the hatred go. She became bitter and non-trusting; no relationship ever developed into a meaningful one. Her life did change forever. Gravity turned her smile-line into a frown but bitterness chiseled the deep permanent contortions into her face. She changed both physically and mentally. When asked about the possibility of forgiving her husband she replied, "No, I do not wish to forgive him…ever!"

Would you even consider forgiving such a horrible and frightening offence?

Is the wife justified in feeling the way she does about her husband?

What if you were the husband in this story? Would you expect to be forgiven?

Do you view this situation as a difficult one?

~~*I'm getting better and better everyday!~~

*** I make right choices**

Outcast

"That son of mine has to go! He'll steal the sweet out of sugar! He done stole my car three times and I'm so scared John, my husband…his daddy is gonna kill'em! We put him out three times before, but… I hate to see him on the street. Smell'n bad and looking awful frail. He says, "Y'all should forgive me"! I don't know about this time! Won't somebody please help me….PLEASE!

My Mind on Kill'n and Kill'n on My Mind!

I was driving up North Avenue heading west rolling to the music blazing on my radio, "Roll Bounce" when I looked to my right I thought I saw him. My heart began to race, my eyes narrowed and I pulled over. Feeling tough, strong, and ready to do this thing, slow rolling I reached under my seat and got my .32 revolver and I quickly cocked the trigger. From behind I saw that big auburn Afro, that high-yellow dirty neckline, and the side of that ugly face. I wanted to pull up close so he would see my face as I unloaded my "gat" on his #@$%#!*&%# gigantic head! My heart began to beat faster and faster, as I knew what I had to do. I continued to pull forward. I squeezed the gun's handle in anticipation and tightened my mouth with a sense of determined satisfaction and revengeful pride. I thought, "You can run, but you can't hide, *Nigga*!" And just as I got in front of him I realized…. It was not him! WOW! That's when I knew I had a real problem!

"Hatred"! I started to pray about my hatred and anger but still I wanted revenge in the worst way. I continued to discreetly look for this man another 5 years with the intent to kill him. Why did I hate him so? What had he done to invoke my rage?

Some time before I moved in with my sister after a terrible heartbreak from an old lover. This was not an ordinary love; I mean this was the love of my life. It was a single-family house with an unfinished attic. I moved in with what scanty things I possessed. I was always a very active person and was currently taking karate classes and I must say I was pretty good. (Smile)

My sister had two children and her boyfriend lived with her. I was in and out, using the back door so I wouldn't bother anyone. I stayed gone a lot. Whenever I came in from karate class I would put my karate gear in the drawer by the back door.

One of our family friends fell on hard times and needed a place for herself and her three children to stay for a while.

There we were living up stairs over my sister in that very small unfinished area.

A few months went by, and for some reason my sister's boy friend began to talk negative about me. They said he would see my karate outfit in the drawer and began to curse and say things like, "Karate my foot, I'll show her "@#*#! I hate that &%**&^ son of a %$#@#!"!

I was very seldom there and I didn't know his intent. Late one day I drove up to the Federal Prison in Sandstone, Minnesota to visit my brother – six hours one-way. When I returned I was tired and extremely sleepy. I rushed upstairs to lie down where space was limited with all the children that were there. I sat in a chair and went fast to sleep. I was awaken by a tall figure standing in front of me, yelling "Get out, get out now!" I sat up in the chair and as I began to stand, the man unleashed several blows to my head. I fell back in the chair, dazed. I got up to chase the big man as he ran down the stairs and out of the back door but I fell down the stairs. Not knowing, I left a puddle of blood upstairs and the children were afraid and crying. I got in my car and drove around the block. I noticed blood all over the dashboard. Then I drove to the police station and an ambulance took me to the Emergency Room where I received sutures to my head.

Later I found out that this man was hoping to get me out of the way so he could date our family friend and he thought I was blocking him. This incident was totally unwarranted! His deadly blows were selfishly and licentiously motivated. He tried to kill me over a "booty call"! He attempted to murder me but I *meant* to, fully intended to kill him. And so I set out to taste sweet revenge, at any cost.

After the near hit on a complete stranger, I determined that I was wrong. Killing him was not my option; after all he had not succeeded in killing me – although he tried. I told myself I was wrong and totally out of control. Logic convinced me that my new way of thinking was right, but my heart, my heart felt differently.

I unconsciously held on to feelings deep inside, so deep that I was not even aware that I still planned to kill this guy. There were a few more times I thought I saw him and I reacted in the same manner. I followed that person until I knew for sure whether it was him or not and I fully intended to get my revenge.

Time indeed heals some things but time did not heal this offence. Emotionally, it was as fresh as when it first happened.

As I began to develop a prayer life, I discovered I needed to forgive. God, in

His ultimate wisdom and grace stopped me dead in my tracks and revealed the Lord's Prayer to me. "Forgive us our trespasses AS WE FORGIVE those who trespass against us." And so, I made a decision to forgive. It was not easy. This man attempted to kill me and that, I thought was unforgivable. But when I made that decision, I should say when I allowed God to place His forgiving power in my heart, a peace came over me, a peace I had never felt before.

Part 2:

Should I...

Chapter 2

Have *you* ever felt a hatred that affected your body, sleep, appetite, or ability to go about your daily routine? Consumed by negative thoughts? Did you ever lie in your bed with tears running down the side of your face and feeling as if your head were going to explode?

There are physical, psychological and behavioral ramifications related to UN-forgiveness. UN-forgiveness does not only refer to the immediate offence-related experience. It also refers to the negative emotions related to delayed experiences that have offended you. Most often these experiences later produce resentment, bitterness, fear, anger and hostility, and the inability to trust. These emotions, if left to run rampant, will produce a stress response that can alter your health and even shorten your life.

Health, ~~that's right,~~ chronic stress directly affects your immune system and can earnestly compromise health. I read of a story about this lady; let's call her Bitterlou. She had a serious lung condition and had difficulty breathing. She was literally on her deathbed. A pastor and his wife prayed for her healing. The anointing was present, but nothing happened. When the pastor and wife went home the Lord inspired them to share some scripture (Proverbs 4:20 – 22 and James 5:14 – 17) concerning health and forgiveness. This lady was very bitter and full of hatred as a result of hurts from a downtrodden and very lonely life. After reading the scriptures that had been given to her, she began to pray and ask for forgiveness. And she became aware of her need to forgive. It wasn't long after she found herself increasingly in a peaceful and restful state of mind. Her countenance changed; she looked more alive and yes, she regained her health. Soon after her peace increased and her mind was rested.

It has been proven that Un-forgiveness can cause many physical problems like ulcers and headaches. In the 1995 Journal of Advancement in Medicine, a study was done disclosing the physiological and psychological effects of compassion and anger. The negative effects anger has on the immune system and the heart is astounding. (scripture)

Un-forgiveness will enslave the one whom is not willing to forgive. It is like carrying a weight, a heavy weight around with you all the time. Can you imagine carrying a deceased loved-one with you everywhere you go? No matter how much you loved that person, the idea of carrying them around once they have died is unthought-of. They will begin to stink and decompose and they're heavy! It is noticeable to others as well as a burden to yourself. It is unsanitary and unsightly. People will think you are crazy. If someone or something is dead, it should be buried. This is what unforgiveness looks like in your spirit man - a living soul transporting **dead waste**.

If you want wellness, you will opt to forgive. If you desire eternal life you will chose to forgive. If *you* want to be forgiven, you *must* forgive.

Somebody said...

My friend and I were having a conversation on this topic of forgiveness. And she shared some intense and specific information with me. The dictionary definition of the word is as follows...

Forgive. *(A transitive verb- Webster definition 1: to give up resentment of or claim to requital for i.e. to forgive an insult. Definition 2: to grant relief from payment i.e. to forgive a debt. Definition 3: to cease to feel resentment against an offender.*

Synonym: pardon.

But many people have their own *working* definitions, definitions that fully surpass any stoic dictionary definition. These are some anonymous voices that express their understanding of….forgiveness.

Expression 1

Forgiveness ultimately means, "I let go of trying to make you suffer like you made me suffer. I relinquish my attachment to my hatred of you." Forgiveness means it becomes unimportant that you hit back!

Expression 2

Forgiveness is another word for untying yourself from someone. The fastest way to free yourself from someone who has hurt you and all associated negativity is to untie yourself from that person's ugliness. Forgiving is something you do for yourself. It is the untying yourself from the hurt and hatreds that binds you to the person responsible for your pain. Forgiveness enables you to take a small step of walking away from the perpetrator.

Expression 3

To forgive somebody is to say one way or another, "you have done something unspeakable and by all rights I should call it quits between us. However, although I make no guarantees that I will be able to forget what you have done, and though we may both carry scars for life, I refuse to let what you did stand between us.

Expression 4

Forgiveness is medicine. It is an antidote for the venom of being wronged.

Refusing to forgive is like drinking poison and expecting the person who hurt you to die.

Expression 5

Forgiveness is a mental health issue. If you refuse to forgive you are letting someone else live rent free in your head, using your "utilities" that is your energy!

Expression 6

Forgiveness for most is a process that can not and should not be rushed and there is no shame in not being able to forgive immediately. Some wrongs just cannot and should not be pardoned immediately. Let the abused woman hold on to her anger for a while. Let the young man grieve his innocence that has been robbed. Let the old man systemic injustice.

Most of us can't from hurt to forgiveness in one single leap. God calls us to forgive and God also leaves room for us to be righteously angry for a while.

Expression 7

When my children were very young someone in our church hurt me badly. I struggled with it because this hurt made me not even want to go to church where I would have to look at this person in the choir and possibly even have to speak to them.

I got into a bible class and began to work through the hurt. I found that I could do nothing about my feelings, but with God's help, I could make a conscious decision to forgive the person. This was the only step that I could decide to take.

I still hurt and I still remember what happen, but every time the situation would come to mind, I would remind myself of the forgiveness I had decided to give.

Eventually, as God continued to work in my life, one day driving down the road I saw how God could use this experience to move me, to grow me up spiritually. Although God had not authored the situation, God had taken the situaion and used it for good. In fact, I felt like Joseph in the bible when he told his brothers, "even though you meant it for harm, God has used it for good."

Suddenly the feelings of hurt were gone. Because of God's grace, I could have hugged that person and told her thank you, you are totally forgiven. I did not because much time had passed from the time the incident occurred.

I still remember the incident, but without anger or hurt. From my experience I don't believe that forgiveness requires forgetting. However, the hurt is healed and remembering is not a relapse.

Expression 8

A few years back, someone committed a horrendous crime against me. I was completely justified in the flesh for hating that person for life! To make matters worst the person was unrepentant. When I tried to forgive this person what came out of my mouth (which was in my heart) was "want him to be dismembered and fed his own body parts!"

Obviously, this wasn't getting me anywhere. All I could think about was this crime and my pain. I knew I couldn't go on in that state of mind.

I will never forget the moment when I was sobbing my eyes out and said, "Lord, I can't forgive this person on my own. Please help me." That very moment, the Lord God Almighty came on the scene and I felt the entire burden of rage , guilt, shame, hatred, unforgiveness and bitterness, everything lift of me in an instant.

The love of God flooded me and I was completely full of His love toward the unrepentant person. I was set free from the anger and the powerlessness this person had brought into my heart. It wasn't anything I could do by my self. I can tell you that forgiveness is not a feeling. It is a decision and a choice. Once I has chosen to be free of my anger and made the decision to forgive, God could work with me. All the hurt and anger is gone completely and forever. God did this for me.

==============================

Nobody's Perfect

My dad was a very fine man. He was considered good looking by many of the opposite sex. He wooed my mother with his charming ways. He wined and dined her, lavished her with flowers and bought her an expensive Hi-Fi. (That is to say, a record player). After he won her heart, he soon began to display abusive behaviors. He did not want anybody to come over to visit. He didn't even want my mom to go to church. He started physically beating her. When I was about 5 years old, I remember one such incident. One very late night, he beat my mom. I remembered it because he beat her so badly she developed amnesia. She didn't know who her children were nor did she know her own name. My dad was about to take her to the hospital but I cried, "No, don't take her anywhere!" I thought he would drop her off somewhere or maybe push her out of the car and I would never see her again.

      That night affected me for the rest of my life! I would never trust a man. After all, he was my father, he gave me insight: my information about how a man is suppose to act and what men did to helpless women. All of us kids were there in the house crying and scared to death! Later I told my mom, "When I grow up, I am going to be a big strong man. I will take care of you and be your "protector"!

I was just a little girl but I did indeed adopt that philosophy, not just for my mother but for all women! I really did try to live out that inner vow. After reaching adulthood I could physically beat any man I came across! And I did! I loved my dad but for some reason, I loved my mom more.

I did not know I was angry with my father. I had internalized the abuse and wasn't really aware why we had a disconnection. I did forgive my dad after I grew up.

As an adult I finally realized that I wasn't angry at my dad, but I was angry at the choices he made. My daddy was a hard working man and torn between situations. He loved two. He loved my mother and he loved his wife. He was an adulterer and he wouldn't forgive himself.

Subsequently he became an alcoholic. He would drink until he couldn't talk. His tongue would become thick as mud. Man oh man, I didn't like that, it frightened me. His behavior made me afraid to be around him.

It was later discovered he was still married when I was born. So I was a "love child". He eventually told my mom the truth. We didn't realize it because he lived with us most of the time. My mom really loved my dad and she favored me because of it. That explained why I felt like my brother and sisters really did not care for me at all.

There were certain things and situations that I was not able to see or understand until I became an adult. And yes, I did have to implement forgiveness to both parents.

Well I know now that my parents were not perfect, and they made many mistakes, but I tell you, I thank God for them.   I really look at my mom as a trooper, a woman with strong shoulders that she acquired from her honored, notable and much loved, Aunt Julia. I feel better about my parents now that I have forgiven them for their mistakes. I'm not sure if my dad ever forgave himself for his blunders in his life. But he did ask God to forgive him.

~~*Love is powerful~~
Show me a family that is not dysfunctional! Then put them on The Oprah Show

---

Proper Perspective

I was watching a Christian station the one-day and I heard this story of a girl who was in college and often wrote her parents who were taking good care of her as they struggled to send her to school. The letter:

Dear Mother,

I would like for you and dad to sit down. Are you sitting? I am sorry it took so long for me to write, but we had a small fire in my dorm and I had to relocate. I moved in with a friend of mine. He was so gracious to let me stay with him without charging me any rent. He is so well mannered I know you will love him as I do. I want you to meet him. Yes we do plan to get married before my pregnancy begins to show. My next doctor's appointment will take care of the S.T.D. that I got from a dirty toilet.
Okay…

Well mom, no I am not pregnant, there was no fire, and I do not have a boy friend. However I am failing History and Geometry. I just wanted you to see things in their proper perceptive.

Love,

Your daughter

Well that got me! (Smile) How about you? Is the glass half full…. Or is the glass half-empty? When you look out the window after a rainy night, what do you see? Do you look down and see mud? Or do you look up and see stars in the clear moon lit sky? Well…?

You're Mistaken

Behind the closed door we could hear moaning and groaning. A high-pitched voice, "No I don't want it!" (Umm, yuck, peyuckh, ah –husk hummock, ok, ok…. nooo no more)". "Come on baby take it like a big girl. You will feel sooo much better. Come on please" The male's voice was begging. We were about to call the police when the high-pitched voice said, "No daddy that medicine is nasty I don't want any more!

And so …how did we feel?

Violence on the evening news…Without it, newscasters would not have a story to catch the interest of their viewers.

Keep in mind forgiveness does not mean reconciliation. The thoughts of vindication… may re-enter your mind on occasion. The act to forgive may go into remission…but reprieve… forgive… forgive!

Chapter 3

Imagine for a moment what it must feel like to be snared in one of the world's most brutally war-torn regions...scared by the harmful aftermath of racial hatred, famine, or civil war. In many cases these men, women, and children have no family left. No food or haven, no escape from the ongoing violence that surrounds them!

Now come back to your own reality. Someone owes you money, you stole my man, he didn't even speak to me, she looked at me funny! You wronged me and I'll never speak to you again, ever in life! How important is all this petty animosity in light of the major and numerous unfortunate situations throughout the world? What would happen if you put your attention on somebody else for a change...feed someone, give someone a compliment, clothed the naked, shelter the homeless, do an unselfish act and for once take your mind off of "your story"?

Studies have shown us that the monster of Un- forgiveness is not invisible. The effects may be delayed but they are real. It affects some of us mentally, spiritually and physically. It can cause physical deterioration, rapid heartbeat, loss of sleep, and constant overbearing thoughts sometimes referred to as worry. Worry can cause ulcers, indigestion, heartburn, hives, headaches, shingles and other aches and pains. Depression comes on different levels with diverse expressions, such as over eating, under-eating, anorexia, bulimia, carelessness, and unconcern. It can cause "fuzzy" thoughts, suicidal ideals and excessive alcohol and drug addictions! Un-forgiveness breaks our spirits. We could go on.

(Proverbs 17:22) *A merry heart doth good like a medicine; but a broken spirit drieth the bones.*

I know a lady who told me of a situation with her husband. As she was telling me, she began to sweat and breathe heavy. Her voice became louder and louder. Her facial expression changed, and became distorted. She told her story with excessive energy as if it had happened yesterday. * *Come to find out, it happened over 25 years ago.*

Forgive
Ok, now is a good time to define just what forgiveness is. Some people have the knowledge but not the language. Let us now examine what Webster's declares. Forgive means; to give up resentment against or desire to punish; pardon; to over look an offense; to cancel a debt. That is clear and easy to

understand, not complicated, simple huh? Well, it has been determined by many and by myself as well…it is not always an easy thing to do.

There is a vast amount of information concerning this thing called *forgiveness*. How to forgive, the effects of UN – forgiveness, and I might say this information is much needed. We all need help in some area of our life. If not now then keep on living and you will one day need some assistance in some area of your life.

So now, should we FORGIVE?

If we want to be free in our minds and *spirit, and experience real peace, we should seek to for-give and be forgiven. Otherwise we will give the offence more power than we realize; more power than its worth. We will give that thing the power and control to occupy space in our minds and hearts, connecting us to constant torment. Forgiveness creates a path and a process toward healing.

I am sure you have heard it said, "I will forgive, but I won't forget." What does that really mean to you? Come on, think about it for a second! Truly, one cannot simply remove the mental imprint of an offense. So, does it mean every time you think of the offence you will seek recompense? Surely you will no doubt always have memory of the things that affected you. That is what memory does, it remembers! You can not justify every wrong nor can you forget every wrong. However, one can chose to forgive and still not have it for breakfast every day. You *can* really forgive an ex-husband or an ex-wife and not re–marry them. When we forgive, truly forgive, we forgive with our emotions. We may remember the deed but the emotional attachment is gone.

I read an article the other day, about a lady, let's call her Patsy... who killed someone, let's call her Meana. They had attended the same high school. Meana had accused Patsy of stealing her boyfriend. You can imagine how high school students can be. They change boyfriends and girlfriends every few months. Many years passed by and they went about their lives and careers. Later Patsy went to the hospital for a simple procedure and died from complications. As it turned out Meana was on staff as a health professional and did intentionally induce Pasty's death.

Looking at that made me realize the repulsive influence of un-forgiveness. It gave me the chills. Just to think how real the consequences of un-forgiveness are Forgiveness is colossal, enormous, immense, and extremely important!

~~Let's do it! Yes I think we should. Forgive!~~

Mother, Father, Aunt, Uncle, Grandma, and Grandpa...the preacher and teachers...everybody makes mistakes! Oh, except for YOU! (Smile) We live the best way we know how. Well there are a few exceptions; I mean there are some wicked people who cause deliberate harm to others. But normally, we don't come out the gate with the desire and aspiration to disarray our lives, or anyone else's life for that matter. Most of your parents did the best they could do, with the information they had to work with along with prior examples set before them. So, should we hold them forever liable for the less-than perfect job they did as parents?

Then we seem to try and prove how much they messed up by further messing up our own lives. Holding on to the negative and constant criticism will rectify nothing. We can break the cycle.

Hurts can be mended and broken things can be fixed or replaced.

Eat this, I mean chew on this! When we forgive, we trade negative emotions like anger, hatred, and hurt for positive ones. We turn into the receptacles of peace, compassion patience and mercy.

Holding on to mental anguish must hurt…and if you continue to hold on to it, it becomes self-inflicted hurt which will evolve into depression.

Living in the present and letting go of the past is very advantageous.

Forgiveness is not elusive. If you want it, you can have it…seek and ye shall find…knock…

Forgiveness will allow you to move forward in your life and not in a Mock -

time – march.   We do not want to march in place, but rather we want to move ahead.   I have heard it said you can't move forward while looking in the rearview mirror!

Part 3:

Could I...

Chapter 4

Before we move forward, ask yourself these questions.

- *Could I forgive after my mom abused me as a child?*
- *Could I forgive someone who is dead?*
- *Could I forgive my uncle for raping me?*
- *Could I forgive him after he beat me over and over and over again?*
- *Could I forgive my cousin for molesting my son?*
- *Could I forgive my pastor who made a blatant pass at me?*
- *Could I forgive my mother whom left me and never returned?*
- *Could I forgive the boy who burned down my house and killed my youngest son?*
- *Could I forgive my dad who committed suicide?*
- *Could I forgive my sister for stealing my husband?*

- *Could I forgive my pastor for hindering me?*
- *Could I forgive my mother for selling my virginity, her own little girl, for hit of crack?*
- *Can I forgive my spouse for being unfaithful?*

Can I Really Do It?

It has been proven over and over that true forgiveness is *possible* and necessary. In order to live a normal life, and to be able to proceed with one's life more productively one must internally be at peace.

No one should allow un-forgiveness to rob him or her and hold them hostage. Un-forgiveness can stunt your growth. Sometime intensive counseling is necessary to overcome the heaviness of un-forgiveness – a slow killer for sure. Some people often do not pursue assistance because of pride, shame or the potential embarrassment it may bring to the family name, what will people say?   Denial is a factor as well. Some may say I don't have a problem." The matter of finances or lack thereof can also play a role in not seeking council. (By the way, there are many places that offer free counsel that information will be noted at the end of this book).

You must know, forgiving someone does not mean that there is no punishment for the offence.

To forgive does not nessasarily mean reconciliation. More about this later... I really would like to emphasize this one fact...it is possible to forgive, even if you don't forget!

Grow Up Little Boy Blue

"Now little boy, little boy, who is yo' daddy?"

"I know his name, and I have seen a picture or two, but that's all! "I hate the nigga!"

And so this boy who is 36 years old, raised by a single mother. A mother who had many challenges of her own, besides the other 5 children all by different fathers! The now "grown up" is still a little boy inside, full of rage and anger. Angry because of the hand life dealt. Who could he charge with this misdeed? How can a boy grow to be a real man without a father image? Who does he look to? He had no role model!

He failed in many relationships by attracting the wrong kind of people into his life. He played around with the girls and with the boys. Trying to control everything and everybody. Lost and confused, he still managed to maneuver through this life. He lived on his own terms, yet without direction. Crying out, but no one could hear him. On the inside he wanted to be a real man! Who can help with this kind of confusion? He could not see God as a father. After all, he had no reference to what a father should be!

This young man with much prayer and guidance from a youth minister with a very similar background finally realized he had to forgive his absent father and the mother who missed the mark. At that point he was released! His inner pain was banished. He took on the real responsibilities of a man. After he forgave his father, his confusion cleared and the healing process began. No longer on the "down low" or playing with young girls lives, he became a transparent brother. As he consulted God, his life took on new meaning.

New role models and a surrendered life to God gave this young man a new start. He is happily married to a wife that loves him and has two beautiful children that look just like him!

Stages…

A number of years ago I was hurt badly by someone. Words were said to me that was so ugly I was dumbfounded. It took three years for me to forgive the person who said them.

The first year, those ugly words ran rampant in my head non – stop; just like a background program on a computer. They ran continually - hot, angry, pulsating and strong. I couldn't even think of forgiveness.

The second year, I was able to think to myself, I need to let this thing go…but I wasn't ready to do this just yet. The words were really starting to lose their power, but they were still tied to my mind because of my anger.

As I went into the third year, forgiveness really didn't take long. I thought, I might not be able to forgive, but I would try to understand. By putting myself into their mindset and trying to understand where they were coming from led me to make a conscious choice to really forgive.

There are times in life we suffer hurts and what we think is betrayal. It is difficult to understand what makes folk behave as they do. Remember, *everybody has a story!* It is truly sad to discover some people are not who you hoped they would be. Some words can affect you for the rest of your life, whether they are true or not. I still carry the ugly words in my head, but they are now dead and powerless. I read somewhere—

You are great; You are nothing! Both statements can be true – which will you believe?

========================

Bitter or Better

All you have to do is grow up and have children of your own!

It was his fault….no it was her fault. Well now they have invented "No fault" divorce. How convenient to adjust and justify EVERYTHING! Well back in the day, men took care of their families.

Many of our black men struggled as their families grew and they created more mouths to feed. But my mom was not satisfied with the mediocre life style that her husband provided. She wanted more; by any means necessary.

While my father held down two jobs, our mother began to take me and my

81

siblings to visit Uncle Lester, a family "friend" so we were told. We went there often while dad was at work. We played in the basement during their visits. He gave us money and took us to McDonalds or out for ice-cream. We loved Uncle Lester.

It didn't take long before my parents began to argue and fight. Loud, harsh, horrible words were exchanged. Me and my two brothers were scared to death. Our "play uncle was more than just a family friend; he was my mother's secret lover. So yes, we were one of those families that had the mishap of the nasty little word – divorce. Our once "happy family" was gone.

Now who was the blame? I loved the ground my mom walked on! My two brothers wanted and needed our dad, who by the way *was* a great dad! He was a good provider, a good cook, he came to all our school functions and he had a genuine concern for us. But his good loving "*musta*" ran out! As an adult I decided I was pissed-off at my mother.

I realized what she had done to my precious father. My mom and dad are both remarried and doing great. My two brothers are also happily married. Oh, I didn't say, well yes I am happily married, to my third husband! I had to go for therapy. I had to forgive my mother before I could go on with my life. She played the role of a harlot. I had no idea I was mad as hell at her. Now all grown up, with children of my own, I can see that there is no such thing as perfect parents. Forgiveness sometimes comes with age, experience and wisdom.

*I am loved
*I am grateful

"When the law of an eye for an eye is in full effect, all men will be blind."
Desmond Tutu

Confession:

While writing this book, a loved one has aroused anger within me. Yes indeed, my dear sister again! What in the world should I do? Does this mean I have to forgive again?

I asked my sister to look after my mother while I went up north to visit our brother. She often declines to share the responsibility to care for our sick mom. I don't know, maybe I'm wrong but I think a once a month visit is not asking too much. It bothers me to no end that my family refuses to show an interest in caring for the woman who brought them into the world. Perception is often a factor in this unfortunate state of family conflict.

And so, I pray (Smile). I must be careful not to put a band-aid over any issue. And then, I forgive.

Chapter 5

What Is This?

Could it be that you have a secret, hidden UN – forgiveness? Could it be that I had hidden UN forgiveness concerning some events that occurred in my life?

Pat had an aunt and every time she came to spend a "sleep it off night" over at her house; she would sleep in Pat's bed and molest her. Well, when Pat became an adult those images would occasionally come across her mind. But she insisted to her knowledge she never held a grudge.

Being so young, she had no idea that she was being molested at the time. As a matter of fact she didn't even think there was anything to forgive. She did occasionally wonder if that had anything to do with her alternative life-style. She had lived a lifestyle of homosexuality and for her, it seemed normal.

"Now that I think about it," she said transparently, "I did have issues with forgiving myself for wasting so much time on the treadmill of homosexuality all of my life!"

Growing up she felt helpless and soon gave in to the notion that she was born that way. "Man oh man"! She insisted for years, "I was placed in the wrong body!"

As an adult she wanted change in her life. Desiring freedom from her life long desire for women, she invited all the help she could get from clergy and prayed often for those desires to go away.

Pat maintained that belief until she got a new revelation in her later years. She said the Holy Spirit impressed upon her heart that she was not born that way but began to practice being a boy-child at an early age. Her understanding was finally clear.

But by the grace of God and His ability to deliver, Pat has been set free from a vicious cycle and a life of bondage, and torment.

Now consider this, she was also raped as a young child, several times, again she didn't think a grudge was necessary, she took the blame and it was something people just never told anyone or even discussed. "Thank God!" she yelled out. "He brought me out with a clear understanding." And so she decided for her own sake to ask for forgiveness for any hatred or UN forgiveness that she might not have been unconsciously aware. After all she would occasionally have thoughts about the things that happened in her life.

As a result she eventually felt it was necessary to ask for forgiveness, and made a conscious choice to forgive the people who inflicted serious offences against her and for the situations in which she had been placed. Forgive what? Let's go pro.

Robert Enright Ph. D. is a professor of Educational Psychology at the University of Madison, Wisconsin (EFI) Enright-Forgiveness Intervention wrote a psychological definition"

"Interpersonal forgiveness is a willingness to abandon one's right to resentment, negative judgement, and indifferent behavior toward one who unjustly injured us, while fostering the undeserved qualities of compassion, generosity and even love toward him/her." Robert D. Enright and Julio Rique (taken from (EFI manual).1984

Forgiveness is defined as:

"...a person to person response to unfairness, which leads the offended side to give up the right for resentment toward the offending person, eventually influencing the development of compassion and care and even moral love toward the other ... forgiveness moral response involving the following major domains of human development: positive emotions (e.g., feeling of empathy), negative emotions (e.g., feelings of anger and resentment) positive behaviors (e.g., altruism) and negative behaviors (e.g ,revenge seeking and finally positive(e.g. ,he / she is a good person, negative (e.g. ,condemnation):thoughts toward the offending person."

Hey, you can talk to your medical doctor and he or she will confirm that forgiveness has healing attributes! Emotions, feelings, desires...oh my! If we allow our emotions, feeling, and desires to direct our lives we would be in serious trouble. You don't always feel like going to work, or fixing breakfast for your children or husband then there can be consequences. There are consequences for every decision. That's why we can not depend on how we feel. For every action there is a reaction.

Have you ever hurt anyone? Has a loved one or anyone for that matter ever hurt you? Have you fully forgiven that person, or are you still holding on to resentment?

It is true that forgiveness is important to begin healing and a peace in your life? How about moving forward in your life instead of backwards, or standing still? So many times we can get stuck in certain areas in our lives. And sometimes we need help to move forward to another level. But first, we must recognize that there is an established fact that a problem does exist. Seeing it for what it is may be uncomfortable at first, but then hope will kick-in and you can transcend to another level in your life.

"The only way to heal the pain that will not heal itself is to forgive that person who hurt you. Forgiving stops the pain and also, stops from return of pain...When you release the wrongdoer from the wrong; you cut a malignant tumor out of your inner life. You set a prisoner free, and then you discover the real prisoner was yourself." – Lewis B. Smedes, Forgive and Forget

---

Chapter 6

Feelings can be very misleading. We must be careful to force them to be subject to rational thinking (Smile)! Here are a few examples: getting up in the morning, by - passing the chocolate, slapping your boss, running a red light, pouring hot coffee on your husband, missing work today, committing adultery, stealing, just to name a few! Have you ever felt any of these emotions?

I heard this lady tell her story…you know everybody's got a story to tell. But will they tell it? Will they share it? Will it help someone?

Well, I heard this lady tell of her story about her long time addictions for she had many.

As she stood there in front of about 50 women in rehab reading the letters that she had written one to her dead grandfather who had molested her many times and she believed her grandmother was very much aware of it. So she wrote one to her grandmother and her mother as well, who was abusive. Not to mention her aunt who frequently told her when she was just a little child… "you *sho'* is ugly". Needless to say this lady that stood there with these letters had little to no self-esteem. Rejecting her own reflections in the mirror, she embraced guilt and shame. She had spent her life looking for love in all the wrong places.

Sadly, this woman developed an addiction to abusive men, alcohol and finally crack-cocaine. She had had eight children that were in the care of a family member during her times of treatment.

She was forced by family intervention into treatment at least 4 times, and each time she relapsed. Her family refused to give up, and resolved that she would not die in the streets.

Many crack addicts were having strokes, heart attacks, overdosing and committing serious crimes due to this monstrous drug.

Remarkably the last time she went into rehab, she was different. Real healing began to take place only after she decided to forgive her offenders, and herself.

The clients were required to write letters forgiving their offenders. She read the first letter as if she hadn't written it. She was cold and unattached! The moderator asked, "Is this you" and the lady stood there about a second. Suddenly she began to shake and tremble and continued; only this time she personalized her experience. The tears ran down her face uncontrollably and with a weaken voice she continued.

Upon completion, there was not a dry eye in the place! The healing had finally begun! Not just for her, but for many of the other people in that rehab facility. They were finally able to tell their own story because prior to this experience the others were not sharing.

After wards they all hugged and kissed and things changed after that. Now over 10 years later she is clean and dry…successful and has a great desire to help displaced women and children. She is currently seeking funding to get a housing to implement her dream. Care for the addict's children and the homeless children.

Write a letter, then burn it up.

My Godmother

Now here's a lady I thought was a little piece of Jesus. She loves the Lord! She lives her life as a woman of God; a bright light shining in a very dark world. She is a praying woman, sweet as a sack of pure cane sugar, and a very loving person. I am so grateful the Lord put her in my life. She makes herself available and I call her to this day and she will pray with me and for me. This woman gives me her honest opinion even when it's not in my favor. I highly respect and love her, my mentor and friend. She has had many experiences in life that one can glean from and grow thereby. She tells it like it is in love. One really never mines being corrected and redirected by that sweetheart. A mature woman of God and a vessel of honor, Elder of her church and my godmother, she shared this story with me about a situation when she had to apply the medicine of forgiveness.

I did notice how sometimes we set ourselves up for disappointments. Not realizing people are human and subject to error I thought all "saved" people were perfect and sinless!

While talking to my godmother I asked her to share with me one of her many experiences with forgiveness.

I took her out to lunch and she began to disclose her story. She worked at the post office for what seem to be forever. Her seniority enabled her to get a desired position of employment and as a result it prevented two other people from being granted a requested transfer. The position was in a quiet and serene place; kind of secluded. The very first night, yes it was third shift she started there, "The Man" was not nice at all; he looked at my godmother with discontent and was not helpful to the new out- of -towner. She would ask him a question and he would reply, "Read the manual!" Wow! He was out-right mean and did not mind revealing his nasty attitude – often clamoring expletives. The phone would ring and things would get busy, but "The Man" would not assist, and would go to great lengths to cause her problems. Well this continued for quite some time. My godmother began to dislike this man and that dislike became stronger until eventually developing into hatred.

Some of us know what it's like to not want to go to work because of some troublesome person or some other situation. So this feeling of hatred didn't set well with my godmother who prided herself as being a Christian woman of God.

One night on her way through the door the Spirit of the Lord stopped her and said, "Pray for those who despiteful use you. So when she got home she looked up the words in the Bible. That scripture stayed on her mind. (Pray for those who despitefully use you)... She began to pray and the more she prayed the worse the man became. He started dishing out mean and nasty remarks every time she came in to work. She went to her pastor and disclosed the situation from A to Z. The advice she received gave her a challenge… She told her to **PUSH**

P Pray
U Until
S Something
H Happens

Pray for him? Ok she began to pray, but was unsure what to pray for. The Spirit revealed to her to pray for his protection and for salvation to come to his household. The more she prayed he became even worse.

So when my Godmother went in to work, she would simply say "God bless you" to the man. She would say those words when she came in or went out.

Now this was a change in itself. She had not done this before.

Her feelings started to change toward "The Man." She began to feel sorry for this guy. He would fall asleep on the job and began to make several mistakes. That eventually caused him to get a pink slip which had him transferred to a different department. *Oh my, will you look at this!*

Well, soon there after "The Man" got very ill and went into the hospital. He asked specifically for my godmother of all people to come see him. *Wow!* She said she was reluctant to go, but went anyway. While there she was introduced to "the Man's" son who had recently gotten saved and they agreed to pray for "The Man." She made a conscience decision to forgive and love this man with the love of God!

While it was not an easy thing to do, she decided to forgive. And God did move on her behalf. Notice how she prayed…Dear Lord bring salvation to "the man's" household. And now you see where the son got saved. She didn't say whether or not he accepted the Lord, but where there are two or three touching and agreeing we shall have it because God is in the mist!

"Self – Image is a factor, if it is concerning (forgiving one's self")
PC, 2006

It is possible to forgive someone who is dead. Remember forgiveness is choosing to forgive. It is a choice. Forgiving is for the offended, more than the offender! (Tuck that in your pocket!)
When you learn the facts about forgiving you will chose it above UN – forgiveness.

Nobody can use a vocabulary that they don't know! Learning the useful words of forgiveness and knowing that it is possible will help some to realize true forgiveness.

My sister aroused anger in me once again. She did not do what she said she would do once again or what I expected her to do. And so this time I really don't want anything more to do with her! And so I had to acknowledge the feelings chose to forgive again and move on! Not Easy…. But, a really good choice.

Forgiveness is not; forgetting, not a condition or absolving, not self – sacrifice, not approving the wrong.

I can forgive and heal!

A very difficult thing to do! There are many stories, true stories that require the application of forgiveness! Decide to do it, just chose to do it!
Forgive…

Part 4:

How Do I...

Chapter 7

Forgiveness is Golden

Forgiveness is Golden, says Lynn, as she shares her skin-chilling story. So often people use the "Lords Prayer" at the beginning or at the close of a program, dinner, ceremony, etc. She went on to say that we should take note, of a very important part, a part that proved to be very important to me. It is the part that reads, *"Forgive us our trespasses as we forgive those who trespass against us,"* **<u>Matthew 6: - 13</u>**.

Lynn goes on to share her convictions, that in this saying, is where we are asking God to forgive us and we should take notice to the twofold request; to be forgiven and we in turn must forgive. A task easier said than done. Whereas Lynn knows this from first hand experience. Lynn has gotten us set as she shares a skin-chilling story from her own personal trauma in her life's journey. Lynn's voice was clear and strong as she began to speak. "As a child I experienced and suffered many cruel abusive, verbal, mental, and physical acts that were imposed upon me! I was sexually assaulted by my grandmother's husband at the age of 10 years old. By the time I was 13 years old I was raped by a man in the neighborhood, that most people called him "a Mad Man." Everybody was aware that he was a serious bully and a threat to the entire neighborhood. Just before I turned 18 years old, an old friend who somehow knew what had happened arranged a meeting with my rapist and I. I was very uncomfortable to say the least. My attacker asked me to forgive him. I told him out right, unreserved, no! He took something from me something I didn't give to him! I didn't want to nor was I able to even consider forgiving him.

Oh my, I found out some years later it was shortly after that confrontational meeting, this guy hung himself. I often wondered, was this a result of my lack of forgiveness! I even felt guilty. I felt a deep sense of responsibility. I didn't know! I felt a sense of great guilt. Definitely!

Years passed and my grandmother's husband lay sick unto death sick in the hospital. I went to the hospital to see him, hoping for a deathbed confession and an apology. It never happened. Somewhere along the line I knew God was dealing with me and in my heart. Nevertheless my life took on increased turmoil.

As a young confused teenage parent, abuse, and removal of my first child from my home and not long after that the sudden death of another child, feeling abandoned in my life I started whoring and drinking heavily. God allowed me to cry out to Him. As He proved He was listening. I sought God, I cried out, "Lord I can't take anymore!" Please forgive me!" God's reply was in this manner, "Consider this my child, should I forgive you for the many things you've done, and you won't forgive people for one single incident?" All this took me to (The Lord's Prayer) I discovered that in our lives we do and say so many things against others, as well as ourselves that would warrant us to go to God and ask His forgiveness, as well as the person or persons that we've wronged. We worry about God's forgiveness and we cannot forgive, or refuse to forgive. We do claim we love God sooo much and can't stand our neighbor. *Matthew 7:12* This is the "Golden Rule" Do unto others, as you would have them do unto you! Yes, I was able to forgive only and I repeat only with God's help. As I chose to forgive. I felt lighter and better and I began to go and grow to new levels in my life. > So be it… "FORGIVE! By; *Lynn*

The price of gold has skyrocketed!

A leader in the community a very wise and sensitive woman, Lynn, … who shared a deeper revelation of some of her life experiences and visions after the interview. I suggested to her to write a book and share and tell. I just believe there are people who need to here that change is possible. There are many that have benefited from Mrs. Lynn's life experiences.

~~*Recite all the affirmations*~~

---

*Affirmation
I chose to forgive.

This will set me free. Free to live and grow on with my life.
I will forgive!

I brought a little hand held tape recorder and asked several people questions about forgiveness. The answers were vast and very interesting some even enormous! But not one did I find funny. Maybe a little scary. Now before I ever did my little research I collected my own thoughts and concepts about forgiveness and I did find that many have a similar concept. I personally believe that concepts and working principals about life come from The "Holy Bible." It's true from cover to cover. It is because human behavior is discussed in the word of God at length, in great depth clearly, and extensively! After all "The Creator" inspired the fingers that wrote the book. The fall of man and the redemption of man…. Who is man that

God is mindful of him…? But if you are looking for a book beside the Bible I suggest you go with someone who has done immense research with well-designed information for your consumption and in terms in which the layman can decipher and comprehend. Some measurable information will be extremely helpful to bring you to an understanding of this thing called *"forgiveness."* However this book is design to do just that. When the direct instructions are followed there will be positive results! 21 – 40 days are when habits are formed. Try it!

Chapter 8

Is forgiveness just something we extend to others? Of course not. There are things that we have done to ourselves and others that require forgiveness. Here is a real situation to take a look at and glean from the end result.

A Seed of Poison

We finally joined a church! I was so happy and elated that now we really do have the perfect family. After all my husband was raised in the church, but somehow strayed away. Anyway, here we are now in church. The people were very nice and the preacher really taught the bible well. I learned some things about the bible I never knew before. I soon joined the choir. I loved it! I discovered I could sing. I practice every day. My vocal cords soon gave me indications of readiness. I can now sing in public.

We now have three boys, Jubug 11years old, he looks just like his daddy, Truman 8years old, very sensitive little runt, and then there's Scott 7 years old he's the tough guy and one precious little girl 5 years old who enjoys antagonize her brothers; yes we named her Precious. We eat dinner together and occasionally went out for entertainment.

I slept well at night feeling good and secure. I was happy as a lark. Yes, I had a song in my heart! We became popular at church as we began to work and stay busy helping all we could help. My husband began to get overtime at work. I was very pleased because we needed the money. Doris one of the sisters at church helped me with my children every Sunday evening. My husband worked closely with the organist, J.J. they became good friends. J.J. would come over for dinner almost every Friday. Rumors began to surface; my husband was seen at a gay bar with J.J. Well, J.J. was a little on the soft side. However, I discounted that noise and gossip. I know my man is a real man!

It was a Tuesday morning I left work early feeling sick. I stop at Starbucks got a hot cup of coffee and rushed home anticipating lying down in front of the TV. As I walked through the door I heard noise from my bedroom. My alarm went off, "back door" it sounded very loudly. As I proceeded my husband came running with a towel wrapped around him, and right behind him soaked wet wearing boxer shorts, J.J.! What in the world…my mind went backwards to a movie I once saw… I could get away with it…I'll kill them both… my mind continued…what people were saying was true after all! As I ran to my closet, where he knew we kept our family protection. My husband running behind me explaining they were working out in our basement gym. I loved him so much and wanted to believe him still I slowed down long enough to slap him across his face with all the strength I had in me. All in the background J.J. was yelling Oh no, oh no, oh no! When my husband realized where I was going, he grabbed me and slapped me. My head hit the table as I fell to the floor. The next thing I remember is waking up in the hospital. Was this really true! I later realized my husband was telling me the truth. My nephew and his dad were also in the basement working out with a new weight trainer.

J.J. had just gotten out of the shower, looking for a towel. Could I forgive myself for entertaining that infectious nasty gossip, a low down rumor, a rumor? I had listen and entertained those infectious thoughts "people" put in mind. Would he ever forgive me? Can I forgive myself?

Well, my husband soon moved out of our home. He moved in with J.J.

Dare To Forgive Yourself!

Do you dare release the person you are today from the shadow of the wrong you did yesterday? This will require courage and a true desire to move to another level in life.
Sad to say it has been noted that many men have had an extra-marital affair and as a result a child came out of it. Common? Some say! Well here is one uncommon some say… anyway, the woman or wife has an affair, and a child comes from it! A white couple and now she is pregnant with a black man's baby. Wow…. How do you forgive that when you got to look at it for the rest of your natural life? At least the woman doesn't have to see the child that the man has

made, all the time. But here it is! What to do…. How can I forgive this? Truly! It will take a God for me to forgive this @#%#&! Ok, so what is he, you know, the man that has done the same thing. Well, yes it will take God to help one to make a real transition into a level of forgiveness and that will require…LOVE!

The first step in forgiveness is to admit and recognize the unforgiveness. > < The second step is to choose to forgive. Make a conscious decision to forgive. > Yes dear, it is a choice.

Simple, right? Not so fast here… to forgive can be difficult, very difficult but, possible and attainable.

I can do this!

Part 5:
Forgive

Chapter 9

Pain & Hurt: This Too Shall Pass

We were together 7years and we had a baby boy and he of course became a Jr. (Smile) but he didn't look like his mother, or me so we thought he would grow to favor one of us. Well, as it turns out he looked like the milkman! Yeah, some dude at the gas station. Blood test proof , (DNA)…the child I fell in love with was not mine. Did I want to kill her? YES! That sent me to my knees talking to a God I never knew before to save me from this heartbreak and rage I had continually growing inside of me. Forgive the hoe! Never! I don't know if I will ever trust another woman. Love don't love nobody. It takes a fool to learn.

Flash forward a few years. This young man's life has changed. He and his new wife attend church and are very happy.

Oh, yes with three children. ~~(Smile)~~ Is his happiness by chance?

***

A Higher Power
~~Could I…really…~~

There was this young man who was active in his local church. He was an usher and he sang in the choir. He had given his life to Christ at a young age and led a happy and a very productive life. He lived with his parents and younger sister. Fresh out of collage he was saving money for a new car and a deposit on a van for the church. One Saturday evening after spending time at the shopping mall, he and his sister came home with a few packages and once inside they made a disturbing discovery. The local crack – head was rummaging through the household belongings. They hadn't noticed the break – in until they were in the house. The intruder spotted them and quickly attacked them. Without a word the intruder grabbed the church going young man, and slit his throat. He instantaneously fell to the floor bleeding profusely. Then the intruder began stabbing his sister. They lay there on the floor dying. The room smelled strange, the stench of fresh blood was prominent. The young man began to pray internally and asked God to save the lives of him and his sister as they lay helplessly on the floor. He somehow manages to get to the phone, and realized he couldn't talk. Fear increasingly overtook him.

The emergency operator was able to trace the address and names of the occupancies. The paramedics showed up just in time to rescue them, consequently saving their lives.

While in intensive care, the doctors informed the young man that his sister was doing fine, but the drug addict had murdered his mother and father prior to their arrival at the house.

This wonderful young man-child was radically broken. He was broken hearted as he grieved in silence the lost of his parents. His very eyes searched heaven for answers. "Why!" Why did this happen? God had always been their protector. Was this tragedy His will? What had they done to warrant this? It wasn't long before anger replaced the gut wrenching grieve, hurt, and pain. He clearly visualized the mad man who had done this to him and his family and he fiercely hated him.

Months passed and the young man-child began to recover of the physically. His only scar would be from the knife wound that stretched across his neck alone with his inability to speak. His vocal cords had been severed from the knife. The doctors said he would never be able to speak again. In silence hatred grew

within the heart of this young man.
Thought of revenge festered, discuss and
repulsion overtook him. He tried to pray.
He put forth-tremendous effort to touch
heaven for help. But it seemed as though
the heavens were shut up. He felt so all
alone, but continued to pray and talk to
God.

It was a short time later the police
apprehended the heartless, mutilating,
murdering, and intruder. The trial was set
and as due process the trial was rather
lengthy. The young man and his sister
came to the courthouse whenever the
dates were scheduled. Their presence was
menacing. Hate emulated from the young
man. He wanted the death penalty and
thought even that would be too kind for
this animal.

He wanted that man to suffer for
what he had done. His mind wondered to
a time when he was singing in the church
choir, and he began to cry bitter

uncontrolled tears at the thought of never singing again.

Prior to the judge-passing sentence, protocol was to that the victims were given an opportunity to speak in the presence of the courts and the perpetrator. The young man's sister simply cried out loud that her parents were taken from them and that could never be replaced.

The young man wrote a statement asking for the full consequence of the law, but the spirit of God had been tugging at his heart all day. All he could hear was, "forgive, forgive, and forgive." The young man thought it over once again over and over in his mind. He thought to himself, how could I forgive this monster?

He killed my momma and my daddy, he cut my throat, and I won't be able to speak the rest of my life. He stabbed my sister in the side. He really tried to kill us. He left us to die! In this young man's mine to forgive was definitely too much to ask. However he continued to hear in his spirit that he should forgive this man.

Finally, the prosecuting attorney began to read the written statement, and as he read the young man had an overwhelming urge to interrupt him. He waved his hand to tell the judge to wait! He wanted to convey that no matter what happened he decided, by faith, to forgive his offender. But no one paid any attention to him as they were engaged in court proceeding.

As they continue to read, the young man opened his mouth and whispered, "I forgive him." Surprised by the sound coming from his own mouth, he said it again, this time much louder" I FORGIVE HIM!" At that very moment began to cry uncontrollable tears. He cried because it was a very difficult decision he made. He cried because God showed up! This young man with the sever vocal cords, shortly thereafter shared his testimony and sang a solo at his local church. The boy can sing! He tore the church up!

Love for God and love for yourself…How about *the love of God?* Because of hundreds of references to love in the bible it is certainly one of the most remarkable books of love in the world! *Greater love hath no man than this… that he lay down his life for a friend.*

Yes, love in the highest degree that God has for mankind and the high regard we should in turn have for Him and others. Just to think that God knows the number of hairs on our head and He knows how many we have lost too! (Smile)

Love is not only one of Gods attributes but (characteristics), it is also an essential part of His nature.

When I was a young child I was taking a bath and my mom came into the bathroom, she looked at me and yelled, "Oh, my goodness!" She frightened me I looked around to see if something had jumped in the tub with me or was I bleeding or WHAT was wrong! She looked at me and said you take a bath just like your father. Mind you, I have never seen my dad bathing before. I look like my dad and I even have some behaviors like him.

My family would often remind me of that fact. Well, why not after all I come from his seed! And we often times hear people say things like, woo, he looks just like his mom or she looks like her dad. Well of course, they are the parents. Recent studies concerning newborns and what travels through the placenta crack mother – is transferred to the child crack baby. And we can plainly see the birthing process is important. (Keep this in mind) so for those of us who are truly born of God the same is true…we should have some of His characteristics. This brings me to my point…

"What's Love got to do with it"? This love is not possible unless we have been born again…. That is born again. Yes we will identify with and take on some godly character. * If we know that He is righteous, ye know everyone that doeth righteousness is born of Him.

The true acid test of being born of God… is substantiated (authenticated) validated, proven…in the word of God, it is so clear we often look right through it. How do we know we are born of God? Not because we are PK'' kids. Not because we were brought up in church or had an experience or got the chills or had a dream. Jesus made it plain to

Nicodemus…. Ye must be born again!

God is love but love is not God we must be careful to filter through irrational slogans. ***(1 John 4:8 &16)** perfect love…How do we know…is it because he or she is a dynamic preacher, a great singer, healing the sick speaks in tongues and can prophecy? No… it is in the gifts! Though I speak with tongues of men and of angels…**1Corinthians 13** Not everyone who says Lord, Lord shall enter in. so can we really know? Yes! Yes! Yes!

*(1John 3:14) we know we have passed from death unto life because we love the brethren, he that loveth not his brethren abided in death. Verse 15 states: whosoever hates his brother is a murderer and ye know that a murderer hath not eternal life abiding in him.

(Luke 10: 25 – 37) check this out read it yourself! Now what does it say to you…. Read it again! Come on one more time!

Now check out my love level after church services, or when someone wrongs me or rubs me the wrong way. Do I have the ability to love? We know by our "Love" Simple Huh…I don't think so, you see many of us second rate this thing called "LOVE" but we see our motives should be love. Love is to be giving, demonstrated. We must will to love in spite of…. For this is the true description of, Agape' love yes the love of God. God chose to love Israel and they continually went a whoreing after other gods!

But God commended His love toward us while we were yet sinners. The will, to love in spite of. The bible tells us to aim for love ***(1 Corinthians 14) *(1 Corinthians 16:14)** let all we do, be done in love. ***(Colossians 3:14)**…above all put on love. ***(1Peter 4:8)** above all, love one another, love covers a multitude of fault. This sounds like sacrifice! We should be imitators of God. **(Ephesians 5:1 –2)**. We should give freely and not make people feel bad about it!

There was a man on his deathbed. He had plenty of money, cars you know Rolls Royce, limousines, penthouse, mansions and servants. None of his **family cared for him, his servants** didn't even like him. And his only request was that he wanted someone to love him! Wow! Look at that!

God willed to love mankind. A people that did not love him. Even after we went whoring after other gods, Baal, idols and constantly falling into trouble and turning our backs on Him.

But God made a covenant with Abraham, and heaven and earth will pass away, before His word fails! God loved us while we were yet sinners, oh yes He gave! God demonstrated His love toward us. For God so loved the world that He gave…

Live …and He loved me…*Died* and He saved me…*Buried*…He carried my sins far away…but, *Rising* He justified and freed me forever, and one day soon He is coming back, glorious day!

Jesus paid the penalty for the sins of the world. Accept Him and live, reject Him and die!

Chapter 10

The Faithful Lady

This lady sang in the choir for 10 years. She was middle aged and very faithful, paid tithes and offering went to bible class too. She was very generous. Giving the children her extra change. Donating to almost every ministry the church was involved with. Then one day, believe it or not she got sick. She had to be hospitalized for two weeks when it was discovered she had sugar diabetes.

Consequently she missed a lot of church she had to get familiar with the new medicine and her diet change. She noticed no one from her church called to see how she was doing. She got mad really mad and hurt. Then she withdrew from going to church altogether. About three months went by and the choir president called her, not to see how she was doing but to retrieve the choir robe! She stayed out of church for the next 10 years. Wow, it took 10 years before she went to somebody's church once again.

Has *"The Church"* ever hurt you? Many have experienced hurt induced by "The Church"! Well, that's what people say when someone in church that caused them hurt or pain or great disappointment, they then associate the whole church body with that pain. Yes, they blame everybody! When the pastor induced an offence, oh boy, then God is accused of being at fault and everybody is fake. (*Them there people* ain't right)!

"Yeah baby, I am a preacher, but I sho, wanta talk to you and my (wyfee) don't have to know nutn'!" For every counterfeit there is a genuine article!

"Them church people, phony, fake, and hypocrites!" What an unforgettable experience! I know this lady who testifies at least twice a year. She tells how the church she once attended, treated her, and she stopped going to church for many years as a result. She got sick and was at home and unable to go to church and no one cared enough to call her. And a year later someone calls her from the church and asked her for her choir robe since she wasn't using it. Wow! Whoooo – wee! She placed the blame on (those church people).

A place where one expects to meet solace, real peace and the joy of the Lord and cooperate worships and praise. There are different levels of maturity in the body of believers. We grow; yes it's a process, but should not reflex the true reputation of the church. For every real, there is a counterfeit! We grow out of our experiences. Persecution will come and as a result, we can benefit and have to implement forgiveness. The church people are not perfect. And everybody that say, they are…may not be. And you do not have to judge an apple tree, for it bears apples, an orange tree…. Produces oranges! Get the picture! I believe, we will have to give an account for the mindless and deliberate hurt we have caused some of God's babes.

One can know church protocol and know how to do church and say all the right things, all the right hand movements and what looks like church stuff and still not have a real relationship with God.

Being born to a set of God fearing people…PK's yes (preachers kids), are not born saved. For all have sinned and come short of the glory of God. Going to church don't mean you are saved, neither getting baptized. Now these things are good and necessary…. But…. *Accepting*

Jesus as Lord and Savior and His finished work on Calvary! You know believe in your heart and confess with your mouth that God has raised Jesus from the dead and ye shall be saved. Once this is done for real and genuinely, a change takes place. Evidence of a new birth becomes apparent.

The true acid test for salvation is the ability to LOVE! Yes that agape LOVE! The love of God...the kind of love...that forgives and yes the decision to love in spite of...yes that comes from God! Then they will know we are Christians by our "LOVE"! Two new commandments and all the rest hang on these.... Love the Lord God with all thy heart mind and soul, the second like unto it ...love thy neighbor as thyself...WOW! Look at that!
(1 Corinthians 13 chapter) More on this love stuff later. (Smile)

I'm getting better and better everyday!

When we chose not to acknowledge God we are at risk for removing any and all perimeters in our lives. <u>Anything goes!</u>

Even though the heavens declare the glory of God and thus leaves us without excuse, some won't believe.

---

would i...should i...could i...how do i... forgive...?

Is forgiveness possible?

"Naw, I will not ever forget nor forgive that fool "Mr. Wendentdell…he lied on me. Naw, naw, baby I'm taking this one to the grave!"
that's what grand - daddy said to big moma as he lay on his death bed.

In the book of Matthew Chapter 18:21 –
22 Peter one of Christ's disciples, came to
Jesus asked the question: "Lord, how
many times shall I forgive my brother
when he sins against me, up to seven
times?" Jesus answered, I tell you not
seven times, but seventy seven"
(Krues,200,p.79)Paul in his second letter
to the Corinthians said that our
forgiveness of others heighten Christ's
willingness to forgive us. If you forgive
anyone, I also forgive him". And what I
have forgiven – if there was anything – to
forgive I have forgiven in the sight of
Christ, and for your sake, in order that
(Satan) might not out wit us – for we are
not unaware of his schemes.

Chapter 11

There is more than one way to skin a cat! Make a list of all the offenders. You know anyone that has caused you any hurt and pain. Next to their names jot down the thing that was done to cause you hurt. Finally write down " I chose to forgive_____ for the thing they did. State I will cross out the debt they owe me and I now chose to forgive

_____.

You will be surprised the power of writing a thing has. This method is practiced often and is very effective. Now you try it!

Take a peek at the 15th chapter of Luke. That is quite the trilogy. And the real bottom line is our loving Father demonstrates "Forgiveness big time"! The willingness to "Forgive. And then He rejoices! God and heaven rejoice when one repents. Change; turn from a negative direction.

The king decided to update his accounts and in the process, one of his debtors was brought in owing him $10,000,000!　　He couldn't pay his debt, so the king ordered him to be sold for the debt, also his wife and children and everything he had.　But the man fell down before the king and with his face in the dust and said Oh sir be patient with me and I will pay you all of it!　Then the king was filled with pity for him and released him and forgave him his debts.

But now when the man left the king he went to a man that owed him $2,000 grabbed him by the throat and demanded instant payment...right now!
The man fell down before him and begged him to give a little more time. But this man would not wait and had the guy arrested and put in jail until the debt was paid in full.

Then the king found out what happened. The king called this guy and said, " you evil hearted man I forgave you and you can't have mercy on others, just as I had mercy on you!

Then the angry king gave him over to the tormentors. **(Matthew 18:21 – 34)** …so shall my heavenly Father do to you if you refuse to truly forgive your brother!

At the end of chapter #1, we mention this statement;

To forgive doesn't mean that there is no penalty. God is a forgiving God and a God of love and a just God! Sin has a penalty and God, being a just jugde will not say, " oh, that's ok you've sinned and I forgive you because I love you. Sin must be judged.

If you commit a crime and went to court, the judge must pass judgement and rightfully apply the penalty.

(Romans 6:23) The wages of sin is death! But the gift of God is eternal life, through Jesus Christ.

(Matthew 6:10 –13) *Our father who are in heaven holy is thy name thy kingdom come thy will be done on earth as it is in heaven, give us this day our daily bread and* <u>forgive us our debts as we forgive our debtors</u>*...and lead us not into temptation, but deliver us from evil, for thine is the kingdom the power and the glory forever Amen*
Now here after the Amen,
 You would think He would go on to the next thought or paragraph…. But look…

(Matthew 6:14 –15)
 14 For if ye forgive men their trespasses, your heavenly Father will also forgive you;

15 But if *ye forgive not men their trespasses, neither will your Father forgive your trespasses.*

Can we delete the word…(if)? It may be better for some of us to remove that little word (if). That word, (if) is causing a problem for some of us. (Smile) and I say think about that just for a moment.

This monumental statement illuminates tremendous light on forgiveness and allows us to really see clearly, how important this forgiveness thing is as we chose to implement it in our lives. Our salvation lie is the balance. That's it…case closed. No body is worth that much, whereas I should lose God's forgiveness because I refuse to forgive. I believe if we took this seriously, we would demonstrate more MERCY! Forgive as the Lord has forgiven us with our perfect selves! (Smile)

(Matthew 18:21 – 35) This parable speaks about forgiveness and if you look at verses 34 – 35 Jesus said, "…and his lord was outraged and delivered him to the tormentors 'til he paid in full. Likewise shall my heavenly Father do also unto you, if you forgive not every one his brother's trespasses? Evoking compassion is a God thing.

(Colossians 3:13) Forbearing one another and forgiving one another, if any man have a quarrel against any; even as Christ forgave you, so also do ye!
If you have an ought against your brother, leave your gift…oh my! How important this thing is!

Somebody is knocking at your door. You have decided not to answer the door. You're relaxed and just don't want to be disturbed. Your shoes are off; you are on the couch or in your easy chair. Someone is still knocking at your door.

You say in your mind, well they've been there long enough, now go away. The knocking is continuous and getting louder. You become upset and in your mind, you call them stupid, but the knocking goes on and on and louder and consistent. Finally you get up and go to answer the door...WHAT IS IT !!!!.... Who is it, why do you keep knocking for? Point is you will answer the door. Such is life! Jesus said...

Seek and ye shall find, knock and the door shall be open unto you...

Will you stop after a few minutes? I say keep on knocking, do not give up now, just on the other side there it is!

From the wisdom of the text.... We must take the two new commandments and all the others fall under them. Look! Look. See see. This is our help! Our help!

Seek and ye shall find! If you are seeking something, that means that you will undoubtedly, spend some energy toward getting information on whatever topic you are seeking. Some people say they are seeking God but will not go to church to hear the word of God. Neither will they peel open the Bible. Some have a welfare mentality and desire some one else to lay information and other things out before them. Step # 1) accepts and admits. Step # 2) learns something about forgiveness… get some testimonials from others. You're not alone you are not the only one who has had incest in the family, you're not the only one that has experienced the tragedy of divorced. You are not the only one that has been, beaten, abandoned, mistreated, lied on, and burned out, lonely, mad as hell, You are not alone!

Chapter 12

Solutions

"I am not impressed by people who get on talk shows and tell of their dysfunctional family and negative situations; show me a functional family, show me the perfect one! Let us work on solutions and interventions! You bring a hammer and I will bring the nails!

I remember this guy said, no one really cares to hear other people problems all the time, and half the time they're glad it's you!"… And that it is not them that are in a situation.

Now you know there are some compassionate people who really do care, and of course God our Father bottles up every tear, understands all our fears… Come unto me all ye that labor and are heavy laden… and I will give you rest! Oh my, what a joy to enter into Gods rest, whooo - weee just to really lean on His everlasting arms…. For real!

You know, sometimes we ask for advice, already knowing the answers. Then we get good advice; some free and some we pay for but do not apply the advice that was given. What in the world is that? Let's get real! You can never fool God.

Salvation?

Have you accepted the Lord Jesus as your personal savior? The Bible states, That if you confess with your mouth the Lord Jesus, and believe in your heart that God has raised Him from the dead, you shall be saved. For with the heart man believes unto righteousness: and with the mouth confession is made unto salvation.*

(Romans 10:9 – 10)

You know, I really hope and pray that this work will or have blessed you. I know you will enjoy a new level in your walk with the Lord in this life.

To grow as a child of God requires some nutrition;

1) *Feed on His word...read your bible everyday!* **(1 Peter 2:2)**

2) *Depend on Jesus He is the light of the world.* **(Colossians 3:17)**

3) *Pray without ceasing...Keep talking to God, and Listen to Him as well* **(Luke 11:9)**

Tell others, confess Him **(Matthew 10:32)**

4) *Do something for others...* **(James 1:22)**

5) *Faith comes by hearing the word of God...go to church!* ***(Romans 10:17) (Hebrews 10:25)***

Some say I don't want to go to church because of all those hypocrites...and sinful people… " All them people ain't right! Well the minute

You walk in, you will know the church is not perfect because you are there. (Smile) That is referred to the Physical church. So then Faith comes by hearing the word of God! That's it! Do not forsake to assemble yourselves together!

<u>For every genuine there is a counterfeit!</u>
<u>So yes there are people who are for real!</u>
They got to copy cat something.

If you have not accepted Jesus as your Lord and Savior…realize

He is the way, truth and life, no man come unto the Father except by Jesus. For all have sinned and come short of the glory of God…

The wages of sin is death, but the gift of God is eternal life through Jesus…JESUS is the way, truth and life! Won't you accept Him in your life today don't delay!

Look at this, *they said He was coming…and He did!*

They said He would be hung on a cross and die…. He did!
They said He would rise again…. He did!
And finally, they said He is coming back… "WHAT YOU THINK"? It has been noted we are in that season where as the Lord is soon to return! Sooner than you think. Now, are you ready? I mean are you ready for His return? The Scripture says make your election sure. Are you sure? You can be! You can know deep in your heart. Forgiveness is crucial, yes a very necessary fuel. No man knows the day or the hour…

But God told us, in and near the end times there would be increase of wars and rumors of wars and earthquakes in different and unusual places but the end is not yet…. After this "Gospel has been preached to every nation then, said the word of God *then, shall the end come!* ***(Matthew 24: 5 – 14)** Please read this portion of the word. Verse 6 say there shall be wars and rumors of war, nation against nation, but the end is not yet. Then verse14 tells us the season of time, after this gospel is preached. *Wow!* Take a look and see what the Lord has to say to your heart concerning this thang! If you want something, you look for it or you do what you must do to attain it. You will find it…if you seek! Ha – ha, oh yes you will! If you seek you shall find!

He, who has ears, let him, or her, hear what the spirit of the Lord has to say to your heart. Speak to my heart Lord! Glory to God!

Her are some serious steps to take. If you are for real, I mean really for real.

1) *Identify…what who and why*
2) *Chose to forgive, despite the feeling of adverse emotions…*
3) *Be informed…don't be tricked by misconception of what forgiveness is not.*

< And now may the peace of God follow you as we pronounce His blessing upon you and your family and loved ones... >
Ok! You thought it was over? Well, I feel that I will give you some more practical strategies that will help. ...If applied! So many times we know the answers and then, we only think about it and not apply them. So it will work if we work it! Wow! I always wondered what that meant. (It will work, if you work it!) These means that you must do it and not just think about it! Some people lie on the couch and watch an exercise program, hoping to lose weight. Some sit and look at the messy house and think about cleaning up and getting organized. But that's it.... They do nothing but think about it! So I suggest to you, do it go ahead and make the conscious choice to forgive.... Put it in action! NOW! And don't delay. Do it today!

1) Get papers and pencil and write it down...
2) pray about it, be specific please
3) Make a conscious decision to for give...
4) Say it out loud; (I forgive myself for... or I forgive John Doe for... Really say it out loud, so that you can hear yourself and that will help allow it to get into your spirit.
5) And now be thankful for, the ability to for-give... (out loud)
6) Share it with a friend, your pastor or counselor ...someone you can trust.
7) NOW, wash your face!

Would you? Well, if you understood the benefits, you would.
Should you? Well, if want to be free and have good results in life, you should.
Could you? Well, if you really want to, you could. True forgiveness is possible!

How do you? Well, it's not a feeling, but forgiveness is accomplished by a decision and conscious choice!

Notes

There should come a time in your life when you can realize, who matters, who never did, who won't any more and who always will, so don't worry about people in your pass. There is a reason they didn't make it to your future.

The best contribution one can make, is self – improvement! Please continue to work on yourself.

P.c.

Bibliography

*All scripture is taken from The King James Version

Florence L. Johnson Ph. D. (Johnson 1990)

Robert Enright and Julio...taken from the (EFI) manual 1984
Forgive and Forget ...
Lewis B. Smedes 1984

About the Author

Born September 28th 1956 a love child. Born and raised in Milwaukee, Wisconsin.

Postlude

Lewis B. Smedes is a professor of Theology and Ethics at Fuller Theological Seminary in Pasadena, California.

You will find in his book (Forgive and Forget) 1984, a Postlude that states; We do it silently, invisible and freely. "when we forgive , we ride the crest of love's cosmic wave; we walk in stride with God. And we heal the hurt we never deserved." Forgiveness is immediate, the healing is a process! I say …Let the healing began. Forgiveness is possible!

APPLICATION   Date

Name------------------------------
        (Last)   (First)

Birthday   /   /

Name of the offender --------------------------

The offence that took place
(Describe in detail)

I make the choice to forgive----
I make a choice not to forgive----------

Sign

<u>Journal My Own Experiences</u>